Fish Stories

By
HENRY ABBOTT

NEW YORK
1919

Preface

AN ALLEGED humorist once proposed the query, "Are all fishermen liars, or do only liars go fishing?" This does not seem to me to be funny. It is doubtless true that a cynical attitude of suspicion and doubt is often exhibited on the recital of a fishing exploit. I believe the joke editors of magazines and newspapers are responsible for the spread of the propaganda of ridicule, skepticism and distrust of all fish yarns, regardless of their source. The same fellows have a day of reckoning ahead, for the circulation of that ancient but still overworked mother-in-law joke.

It is quite possible that some amateur fishermen, wishing to pose as experts, are guilty of expanding the size or number of their catch, upon reporting the same. But I cannot conceive of a motive sufficient to induce one skilled in handling the rod to lie about his fish. The truth always sounds better and in the case of a fish story, truth is often stranger than any fish fiction.

In my own experience and observation I have found that the more improbable a fish story sounds the more likely it is to be true. The in-

3

credulous attitude of the average auditor, also, is discouraging, and often reacts against himself, as thus some of the very best fish stories are never told. To me, it seems a pity that through these Huns of history many charming and instructive tales of adventure should be lost to literature and to the unoffending part of the public.

The fellows whose exploits are here set down, seldom mention their fishing experiences. They are not boastful, and never exaggerate. They do not speak our language. I have, therefore, undertaken to tell their fish stories for them.

H. A.

4

Fish Stories

by

Henry Abbott

BIGE had the oars and was gently
and without a splash dipping
them into the water, while the
boat slowly glided along parallel to the
shore of the lake. We had been up
around the big island and were crossing
the bay at the mouth of Bald Mountain
Brook, which is the outlet of the pond
of that name, located in a bowl shaped
pocket on the shoulder of Bald Mountain
three miles away. I was in the stern
seat of the boat with a rod and was casting toward the shore, hoping to lure the
wily bass from his hiding place under
rocky ledge or lily pad, when I discovered another and a rival fisherman.

He was operating with an aeroplane
directly over our heads and about two

The Osprey

hundred feet above the lake. Slowly
sailing in circles, with an occasional lazy
flap of wings to maintain his altitude,
and at intervals uttering his sharp,
piercing, hunting cry, the osprey had a
distinct advantage over us, as with his
telescopic eye he could penetrate the
lake to its bottom and could distinctly
6

see everything animate and inanimate in the water within his hunting circle. He could thus, accurately, locate his prey, while we could not see deeply into the water and were always guessing. We might make a hundred casts in as many places, where no bass had been for hours. So I reeled in my line, laid the rod down in the boat and gave my entire attention to watching the operations of the fish hawk.

For about ten minutes the aeroplane fisher continued to rotate overhead; then I observed that the circles were smaller in diameter, and were descending in corkscrew curves, until from a height of about fifty feet the body of the bird shot straight down and struck the water about twenty-five yards from our boat with the blow of a spile driver's hammer, throwing a fountain of spray high into the air. For a few seconds nothing was visible but troubled waters;

7

then appeared flapping wings and the floundering shining body of a big fish, lashing the water into a foam, through which it was difficult to see whether bird or fish was on top. Suddenly, both disappeared under water. Bige excitedly yelled, "He's got his hooks into a whale of a fish! He'll never let go! He'll be drowned! Gosh!!" Then he rowed the boat nearer to the place of battle. A few heart beats later, and the fight was again on the surface. Wings flapped mightily, fish wriggled and twisted and again the water was churned into foam. We now plainly saw the two pairs of ice-tongs-talons of the bird, firmly clamped on the body of the pickerel, which exceeded in length (from head to tail) about six inches, the spread of wings from tip to tip. Wings continued to pound air and water but the big fish could not be lifted above the surface. One more desperate pull

8

on the pickerel's fin-shaped oars and the
bird went under water for the third time,
but with his wicked claws as firmly
clamped into the quivering body as ever.
Coming to the surface more quickly the
next time; the osprey swung his head far
back, and with his ugly hook shaped
beak struck the fish a mighty blow on
the back of the head. The pickerel
shivered, stiffened, and lay still.

The fight was over, but the panting
hawk still hung on to his victim.

Recovering his breath in a few minutes, the bird spread his wings and with
much flapping, laboriously towed the
dead fish along on the water across the
lake, where he dragged it up on a sand
beach. Here he sat for a long time,
resting. Then with his hooked beak he
carved up that pickerel for his stren-
uously acquired meal. I have many
times seen hawks catch fish, but on all
other occasions they have been able to

pick up the struggling fish and fly away
with it. This fellow hooked onto a fish
so big he could not lift it.

FOUR miles up the river and about
five miles eastward over Bear
Mountain, brought Bige and me to
"Hotel Palmer" on the shore of Sargent
Pond. One room and bath were avail-
able and we took both, the latter in
the pond.

We had just enough time to finish
supper before dark. The dishes had to
be washed by lantern light. In the
middle of the night we heard a "Porky"
crawling over the roof, dragging his
heavy spine covered tail over the boards.
It sounded like the scraping of a stiff
wire scratch brush. We heard him sniff
and knew that he was seeking the food
in our pack basket, which his sensitive
nose told him was somewhere near. We

Hotel Palmer

hoped he would become discouraged and go away, but he continued his explorations over our heads a long time, interfering with our efforts to sleep; so a lantern was lighted and we went out and threw sticks of wood and stones at him.

The porcupine came down that roof in the same manner that he comes down a tree trunk, tail first, but the roof boards were steep and slippery and his toe nails would not stick as they do in the rough bark of a tree, so he came down hurriedly, landing with a thud on a rotten log at the back of the cabin. In the morning we discovered that a lot of porcupine quills were sticking vertically in the log so that a section of it resembled an inverted scrubbing brush.

Hotel Palmer was built several years ago, by George, Dave and Leslie. When the law respecting camps on State lands became effective, it was torn down. But

12

on the occasion of the porcupine incident, it was open for the reception of guests by permission.

After breakfast, we found Dave's boat hidden in the bushes in the specified place. During the day we hunted and got several partridges which we proposed to roast later. That evening after supper, while Bige was cutting some firewood, I took the boat and my rod and went out on the pond to get some trout for breakfast.

It was just as the sun was dropping below the western hills, and there was a gorgeous golden glow in the sky. The breeze had dropped to a gentle zephyr that hardly caused a ripple on the surface of the water, so I allowed the boat to slowly drift while I was casting. A tree had fallen into the pond, and sitting in its branches near the tree top, close to the water and about fifty feet from the shore, I discovered a coon. He,

13

also, was fishing, and I was curious to learn just how he operated.

I soon found that the coon was not without curiosity since he, just as eagerly, was watching my operations. As the boat slowly approached the treetop his sharp, beady eyes followed the movement of my flies as the rod whipped back and forth. It occured to me that he might be seriously considering the advisability of adopting a fly rod for use in his fishing business.

Just as the boat passed the treetop and but a few feet from it, a good sized trout appeared at the surface and with a swirl and slap of his tail grabbed one of my flies and made off with it toward the bottom. Instantly the coon became very excited. His body appeared tense; his ring-banded tail swished from side to side; his feet nervously stepped up and down on the tree branch, like a crouching cat who sees a mouse ap-

14

The Coon

proaching, and his snapping eyes followed the movement of my line as it
sawed through the water while the fish
rushed about, up and down, under the
boat and back again. And when the
trout made a jump above the surface
and shook himself, the coon seemed to
fairly dance with joy. Presently, the

fish, now completely exhausted, appeared at the surface lying on his side, while I was reeling in the line; when the coon slipped into the water, grabbed the fish in his mouth and swam ashore. Climbing up the bank he turned, grinned at me and went into the bushes with my trout, now his trout, in his mouth and about three feet of leader trailing behind.

BILL stood four feet three inches in his stockings, and if Bill had ever been on a scale, he would have tipped it at seven pounds and six ounces. Bill's body was about the size of a white leghorn hen. He was mostly legs and neck.

Abe Lincoln once expressed the opinion that "a man's legs should be long enough to reach the ground." Bill was a wader by inclination and of necessity. Long legs were, therefore, required in his business, and having begun life with a pair of long legs, Bill's body was mounted, so to speak, on stilts, high in the air, and he found it necessary .to grow a long neck so that when he presented his bill it might reach to the ground. This long neck was ordinarily carried gracefully looped back above his body in the form of a letter S. On the rare occasions when Bill straightened this crooked neck of his, it shot out with the speed of an electric spark, and he never was known to miss the object aimed at.

At the upper end of Bill's long neck his small head was secured, and from it drooped an eight inch beak, which opened and closed like a pair of tailor's shears.

Bill wore a coat of the same color as a French soldier's uniform and his family name was Heron—Blue Heron. Bill had cousins named Crane and he was distantly related to a fellow who, with

Bill

queer family traditions, paraded under the name of Stork.

Bill did not belong to the union; he worked eighteen hours a day. His operations, chiefly, were conducted in a shallow bay where a brook emptied into the lake, directly opposite our cottage. There, Bill might be seen during the season, in sunshine and in rain, from long before sunrise until late at night, standing in the shallow water near shore in an attitude which he copied from a Japanese fire screen; or with Edwin Booth's majestic, tragedian stage tread, slowly wading among the pond lily pads and pickerel grass; lifting high and projecting forward in long deliberate strides, one foot after another; each step being carefully placed before his weight was shifted.

Though an awkward appearing person by himself, in a landscape Bill made a picture of symmetry and beauty and his march was the very poetry of motion.

Bill had very definite opinions concerning boats. He knew that they were generally occupied by human animals, of whose intentions he was always suspicious. Either through experience or inherited instinct, he seemed to know exactly how far a shot-gun would carry.

19

Bige and I never had used one on him
and we seldom had a gun up our sleeve
while in a boat, but Bill never allowed
us to approach beyond the safety line.

Day after day through many seasons
Bill has stood and observed our boat
cross the lake. Without moving an
eyelash he would watch our approach
until the boat reached a certain definite
spot in the lake, when with slow flap of
wide spread wings he lifted his long legs,
trailing them far behind, while he flew
up the lake behind the island. As soon
as we had passed about our business,
Bill always returned and resumed his
job of fishing at the same old stand,
where he "watchfully waited" for something to turn up.

Bill was the most patient fisherman I
ever knew. Neither Mr. Job nor Wood-
row Wilson had anything on Bill. His
motto seemed to be, "all things come to
him who can afford to wait."

20

Early in the season Mrs. Bill was busy with household duties. With coarse sticks, brush, mud and moss, in the dead branches of a tall pine, she built the family nest and laid the family eggs. She also sat upon those eggs, with her long, spindly legs hanging straight downward, one on either side of the nest, as one might sit upon a saddle suspended in mid-air. When the brood of young herons were hatched and could be left alone, the mother also went fishing with Bill, and toward the end of the season the young birds were on the job with mother and dad.

One day early in the season, Bige and I were crossing the lake. It was about ten o'clock. Bill had been watchfully waiting at his old stand since 3:30 A. M. One eye was now turned on the approaching boat, but the other eye continued its search of the waters for the long delayed morning meal. About this

21

time, a yellow perch who also was hunting a breakfast, discovered a minnow who had strayed into deep water far from his home. Perchy immediately gave chase, while the alarmed minnow swiftly darted toward safety in his birthplace under a clump of pickerel grass near the shore. As they passed our boat, the race was headed straight for a pair of yellow legs a few rods away.

Ten seconds later, a snake like neck uncoiled and straightened while an opened pair of shears, with lightning speed descended into the water. When they lifted, the shears were closed across the body of a half pound yellow perch. Bill thus held his fish an instant, then tossed it in the air and it descended head first into his wide open mouth. A swelling slowly moving downward marked the passage through a long gullet into his crop, of a breakfast that six and a half hours Bill had been patiently fishing for.

22

"Sufferin' Maria!" exclaimed Bige, "What a lot of pleasure Bill had swallowing that kicking, wriggling morsel of food down half a yard of throat."

BIGE and I had been spending the day at Moose Pond. Going over early in the morning, we went up the river about five miles, then followed the tote-road around the western side of the mountain to an abandoned lumber camp near the pond. This road had not been used for lumber operations for ten years or more, but it still made a good foot path, though to reach our destination it led us a long way around.

Returning late in the afternoon to Buck Mountain Camp, where we were then staying, we decided to go directly over Moose Mountain, by a shorter route, though the walking through the lumbered section of the woods would be more difficult. In the bottom of

23

the valley between the two mountains, we crossed West Bay Brook. This brook we had fished three or four miles below, near where it emptied into Cedar Lake, but in this section where the stream was small, overgrown with alders and covered with "slash" from the lumber operations, we had not thought it worth the effort.

There was an elbow in the brook at the place where we crossed it, and a large tree lying across the stream had collected driftwood and formed a dam above which was a deep pool about thirty feet in diameter. Looking down from the bridge which the west wind had made for us to cross upon, we saw that the pool was alive with trout. The bottom seemed black with a solid army formation of fish, lying close together, sides touching, heads up stream; while schools of smaller trout, disturbed by our presence, swiftly swam around the pool

24

Dinner at Buck Mountain Camp

reflecting the bright sunshine in brilliant rainbow hues. The scene was one to arrest the attention of the most casual observer, and Bige and I lingered long upon the bridge watching the movements of the hundreds of inhabitants of this natural aquarium.

On the way back to camp we discussed the possibilities of fishing this pool, deciding upon the best place of approach, where one could be partially concealed by bushes while casting. We spent all of the following day marking a trail down the mountain and across the valley, about three miles, from camp to the pool, cutting brush and clearing out a path; then one day when the weather conditions were favorable, Bige went out to headquarters to bring in some food supplies and I, with a fly rod, went down over our new trail to catch a few trout in a pool that had never been fished.

Cautiously approaching, when near the brook, I heard sounds of splashing in the water. Creeping on hands and knees, then slowly on stomach, I reached a position where, through the bushes, the surface of the pool came into view, when, crawling up the opposite bank, I saw a long, slender, shiny, water soaked, fur coated body which was surmounted with a cat-like head; the legs were so short they were invisible and the body appeared to drag upon the ground, while a tapering tail about a foot long followed in the rear. The Otter, including tail, was about three feet long and he had a trout in his mouth which he deposited on the ground and immediately slid down the bank and disappeared under the water. In less than a minute he crawled up the bank again with another fish in his mouth, which was dropped by the first one and the operation was repeated.

27

I do not know how long the otter had been fishing when I arrived, but I watched him work fully fifteen minutes, when he came to the surface without a fish. He then deliberately surveyed his catch, appearing to gloat over it, after which he started down stream, tumbling in and climbing out of the water as far as he could be seen and I heard him several minutes after he had gone out of view.

Coming out of my cramped position of concealment, I crossed over on the fallen tree and saw scattered over the opposite bank literally scores of trout, large and small; some had their heads bitten off, others were cut in half, all were mutilated. Obviously, the otter had eaten his fill and then had continued to fish just for the joy of killing, like some other trout-hogs in human form, such as we all have met.

I went back to camp that night with-

The Otter

out fish. We visited the pool later,
several times, but never got a rise and
never saw another trout in that hole.
The otter had made a perfect and complete job of it. There was not left even
a pair of trout for seed.

A TWENTY inch pickerel of my acquaintance, one day swallowed his grandson. This was an exhibition of bad judgment on the part of Grandad Pickerel. The mere fact of killing his near relative was not in itself reprehensible, since, if all pickerel were not cannibals they would soon exterminate from streams, ponds, and lakes, fishes of all other species. But this particular "pick" was a husky youngster, and while he might very properly have been bitten in half, or have been chewed up into small pieces, the older fish got himself into trouble when he swallowed the kid whole.

A few hours after the occurence mentioned above, the elder pickerel, at one end of a trolling line, climbed into our boat; Bige, who had the other end of the line, assisting him aboard.

"Sufferin' Mackerel! Well by Gosh!! He's got a rudder on both ends; he can

30

The Pickerel with two rudders

swim both ways without turning around, like a ferry boat," commented Bige, as we examined the floundering big fish, which had the tail end of a smaller fish protruding three inches beyond his snout, while the head of the younger was in the pit of the stomach of the elder pickerel.

I have heard and read many tales, illustrating the voracious appetite of pickerel. Boardman in his book, "Lovers of the Woods," tells how his guide, George, while fishing in Long Lake, lost his Waterbury watch overboard. Several days later, he caught a big pickerel and in dressing it found his watch inside, still running. It seems that a leather thong attached to the watch was wrapped around the winding crown and the other end of the thong was looped over the fish's lower jaw and hooked onto his teeth, so that whenever the pickerel opened and closed his mouth the watch was wound half a turn, and thus was kept running.

Not being an eye-witness, my testimony regarding this incident would not be accepted in a court of law. However, I have known pickerel to swallow frogs, crawfish, mice, sunfish and yellow perch with their prickly dorsal fins, young shelldrakes and gulls, and even bull-heads having three rigid horns with needle points projecting at right angles to the body, any one of which horns, it would seem, might pierce the anatomy of the pickerel. Somehow, they appear to get away with all these things, and more.

The pickerel has a large mouth and a multitude of teeth on both upper and lower jaws, in the roof of his mouth, also on tongue and palate. These teeth are long and sharp and they slope inward; some of them also bend down to allow objects to pass into the throat, but they effectually prevent ejecting

33

anything that has been swallowed. So, Grandad Pickerel, if he had regrets after swallowing a member of his own family, found it impossible to throw him up, as the Good Book says the whale cast up Jonah.

Bige and I found we could not separate the two fishes without first performing a surgical operation. In doing so, we also released a shiner which had been swallowed with Bige's trolling hook and was wedged in the throat alongside the smaller pickerel. This was the most amazing part of the incident, and proves the gluttonous character of the pickerel and his complete inability to appreciate the limits of his own capacity.

We found upon examination that the process of digestion was operating, and that the head of the smaller pickerel was nearly dissolved in the stomach of the larger fish. Another hour, and grandson would have slipped down an inch and the process of digestion would have been repeated upon another section.

A white man cuts his fire wood the proper length to use in his fireplace. An Indian puts one end of a long branch or sapling into his fire, and when it has burned off, he moves the stick in and burns off another section, thus conserving labor.

Our pickerel was digesting his food Indian fashion, or, so to speak, on the installment plan.

BIGE and I were hunting. I was placed on a "runway" on the bank of a small stream which was the outlet of Minnow Pond. Bige had gone around to the opposite side of the mountain and planned to come up over the top and follow the deer path which ran down the mountain side, into and through an old log-road which had not been used for lumber operations for fifteen years, and which was now overgrown with bushes and young spruce and balsam trees. This log-road followed the windings of the brook down the valley to where it emptied into the lake, and where the logs were dumped into the water and floated down to the mill.

Many years ago, when it was the practice to hunt with dogs, the deer acquired the habit of running to the nearest water, where, by wading or swimming they could throw the dogs off the scent. Thus all deer trails or run-ways lead, sooner or later, to a stream, a pond or lake, where the deer has a chance of evading pursuit of his natural enemy. Now, while the game laws forbid hunting deer with dogs, and while dogs are not allowed to enter forests inhabited by deer, yet the inherited instinct of self-preservation of the latter persists, and whenever alarmed by the appearance of man, who in the mind of a deer is still associated with his other enemy—the dog, he immediately starts down his trail to the nearest water.

It was Bige's hope to "scare up" a deer on the other side of the mountain and drive him down the run-way past my watch ground, while it was my job to shoot him as he passed by.

The fallen tree on which I sat was on the bank of the brook and about ten feet above the water, while in the opposite direction, through an open space in the bushes, I had a clear view of the run-way about twenty yards distant.

Time passes slowly in the woods, when one is waiting for something to turn up. Also, it is essential that one sit quietly and make very few false motions when watching for a deer to approach. I had been sitting, with rifle across knees, what seemed a long time. The noises of the woods which suddenly cease when one

walks through the forest, gradually returned. A wood-pecker started up his
electric hammer and resumed the operation of drilling a deep hole into a pine
stub a few rods away. A blue-jay made
some sarcastic remarks about "Caleb"
and then began swinging on his gate
and creaking its rusty hinges. A red
squirrel overhead, made unintelligible,
but evidently derisive remarks about the
intrusion of strangers, and then proceeded to cut off spruce cones and tried
to drop them on my head. A king-
fisher flew up the brook and shook a
baby's tin rattle at me as he passed. An
old hen partridge down the log-road was
advising her children to "Quit! Quit!
Quit!" but her chicks, who were now
more than half grown, paid not the
slightest attention to her warning but
continued picking blue-berries just as
if there were no enemies within a hundred miles. An owl on the limb of a tall

birch demanded, in stentorian voice, to know "Who? Who? Who in — — —" Another fellow, way down the valley responded that he "could!", that he had a chip on his shoulder and that if any blanked owl knocked it off he "Would Who? Who in — — are you anyhow?" Thus the belligerents fought their battle at long range with language, like many other pugilists. A rabbit, who in another month would throw off his brown vest and put on his white winter overcoat, went loping past, stopping occasionally to nip off a wintergreen leaf. These, and other sounds indicating various activities of wood folk, continued to divert attention while two hours passed.

The "Yap, Yap," of a red fox sounded down the brook. A few minutes later his voice was heard again, nearer; presently he came into view. He was wading in the shallow water of the brook, eyes intently fixed upon the water, following a school of minnows. Stepping high and cautiously, he, from time to time, suddenly jabbed his muzzle into the water and brought up a fish from two to three inches long, which he chewed and swallowed with seeming satisfaction. When he missed, which happened often, he repeated his impatient "Yap, Yap" and moved up stream where was another bunch of minnows.

This was the first time I had ever seen a fox fishing and I was intensely interested in his operations. About this time, I heard a commotion in the bushes behind me, and turned in time to see the horns and white tail of a deer over the tops of the bushes as he bounded along down the runway. I heard him for a full minute, still going strong down toward the lake.

Five minutes later Bige appeared, coming down the path gently demanding, "Why in time didn't you shoot that deer? I've been following him for an hour. Fresh tracks all the way. Heard him twice. He went right by here, kicked up the dirt at every jump. You won't get a better shot in ten years. What in tunket were you doing anyhow?"

"Who, me? Why-I-I was fishing."

"BUTTERMILK FALLS" is one of the show places in our neck of the woods. The guide books make mention of it, and the tourist and "one week boarder" see it first. Also, when one tires of fishing, of mountain climbing, of tramping, and is in need of some new form of diversion, there is always "somethin' doin' at the falls." In the presence of their majestic beauty, and in the roar of their falling, tumbling, foaming waters, deer seem to lose their natural timidity and often, in mid-day, show themselves in the open to drink of the waters at the foot of the falls and

41

to drink in the beauty of the picture. In the course of my wanderings in the forests, I have often observed, in spots that are particularly wild or picturesque, or that have an extensive outlook, evidences that deer have stood there, perhaps stamping or pawing the ground for hours at a time, while they enjoyed the view. Such evidence points to the theory that wild deer not only have an eye for the beautiful in nature, but that they manifest good taste in their choice of a picture.

One day two black bears were seen feeding on the bank of the river just above the falls. A family of beavers have built a house about a hundred yards below the falls and have made several unsuccessful attempts to dam the rapids, in which operations about an acre of alder bushes have been cut and dragged into position, only to be carried down stream by the swift waters. This is the only family of beavers I ever met who are not good engineers.

There is also the typical tale of the *"big trout*—a perfect monster of a fish," that lives in the deep pool under the falls. Scores of people have "seen him;" every guide and every fisherman who has visited this region has tried to catch the "wise old moss-back." Several times he has been hooked, but the stories of lost leaders and broken tackle that have been told would fill a volume, and he still lives.

Also, the falls are not without their romance. Tradition, dating back to the Indian occupation, perhaps a hundred and fifty years ago, tells of a beautiful Indian maiden who was wont to meet her lover at midnight when the moon was full, at a spot just above the falls. Coming down the river in her birch-bark canoe, the maiden would await the arrival of the young warrior, who

43

was of another and a hostile tribe, living the other side of the mountain. When the moonlight shadow of the tall pine fell upon a particular spot on the big rock, the ardent lover arrived, guided through the dark and trackless forest by the roar of the falls, which could be heard beyond the mountain top.

Of course the chief, the girl's father, objected to the attentions of this enemy lover, as also did other and rival admirers of her own tribe.

On a mid-summer night the lovers parted, he to go on a mission to Montreal, which then involved a long, difficult and dangerous tramp through the wilderness. Both were pledged to meet again at the falls at midnight of the harvest-moon. As the shadow of the September moon fell upon the midnight mark on the big rock, the Indian maid arrived in her canoe, but the lover came not. Instead, appeared one of the rival

44

Buttermilk Falls

warriors of her own tribe, who told of an ambush, of a poisoned arrow and of a dead lover.

The heart-broken maid then drifted out into midstream and with her canoe passed over the falls and was killed on the rocks below. Tradition goes on to relate how, at midnight of every harvest moon since that tragic event, the ghost of the beautiful Indian maiden appears in her birch bark canoe and sails over Buttermilk Falls, disappearing in the foaming waters at their foot.

For many years I have tried to persuade Bige to join me in keeping the date with this ghost, but up to the present writing it has never been convenient.

Sitting, one day, at the foot of the falls, I was studying the high-water marks on the adjacent rocks, indicating the immense volume of waters that pass over the falls and down the rapids during the freshets caused by melting snows and spring rains, trying to imagine how it might look on such occasions, when a million logs, the cut of the lumbermen during the previous winter, were let loose and came crowding, climbing, jamming, tumbling over one another down through the ravine and over the brink with the mighty rushing waters.

The ground about where I sat was strewn with rocks, boulders and smaller stones, all worn by the ceaseless action of the waters, many of them smooth, others seamed with strata of quartz, granite or sandstone, some curiously marked and grotesque in shape.

As I sat thus, meditating, one of these curiously marked stones, about the size and shape of one of those steel trench hats worn by the "doughboys" in the late war, which had been lying close to the edge of the water and partly in it, suddenly jumped up and appeared to stand on four legs about six inches higher than it had been lying. The legs seemed to be stiff and the movement was like the rising of a disappearing cannon behind the walls of a fort. Instantly there appeared a fifth leg or brace at the back which pushed the rear edge of the trench hat upward and tilted it toward the water, when a telescopic gun shot out from under this curious fighting machine and plunged into the water. An instant later this telescopic gun lifted a small trout out of the water, bit it in half, and with two snaps swallowed it. The telescope then collapsed, the gun-carriage slowly settled back, the tail brace curled up under the rear, the head was drawn under the front of the shell, and the turtle's eyes closed to a narrow slit. Again he looked like the stones among which he lay, but his trap was set for another fish.

In a few minutes another young trout

The Turtle with his trench hat

strayed too close to the shore and the operation was repeated. The manoeuver, though awkward, was swift and every time a fish was landed.

The turtle is a good swimmer and he remains under water a long time. He doubtless also catches fish while swimming. This, however, was the first time I saw him fishing from the shore.

SALMON RIVER is a swift flowing stream having an average width of fifty feet, narrowing as it passes through gorges and having a number of wide, deep pools in which the larger trout collect.

I have made diligent inquiry as to the reason for this name, and have arrived at the conclusion that it was called Salmon River because there were never any salmon in it, but there should be.

About three miles up stream, the beavers have built a dam across it, backing the water up through a swampy section about a quarter of a mile, flooding both banks of the river through the woods, thus creating a fair sized artificial pond.

Bige and I decided that this would be a good place to fish, but that it would be difficult, if not impossible, to reach the deep water of the channel without a boat. So it was arranged that Bige should take the basket containing food and cooking utensils up over the tote-road, leave it at the beaver dam, then go on to Wolf Pond where we had left one of our boats, and carry the boat back through the woods to the dam where I should meet him about three hours later.

In order to make use of the time on my hands, I put on my wading pants and hob-nailed shoes and proceeded to wade up stream, making a cast occasionally where a likely spot appeared. It was a wonderful morning. The weather conditions were exactly right for such an expedition. I passed many spots that would have delighted the soul of an artist. He, probably, would have taken a week to cover the distance I expected to travel in three hours.

I had gone more than half way to the dam, had a few fish in my creel, and was approaching an elbow in the stream. A high point of land covered with bushes shut off my view of a deep pool just around the corner, in which I had many times caught trout. As I came near this bend in the river a most extraordinary thing occured. I distinctly saw a fish flying through the air over the top of the clump of bushes on the point. A flying fish is not an unheard-of thing, indeed I have seen them several times, but not in the mountains, not in these woods, where there are fresh waters only. Flying fish of the kind I know about are met in the Sound and in bays near the

52

Wading Salmon River

ocean. Also, the fish I just then had
seen flying above the bushes, did not
have the extended wing-like fins of the
orthodox flyer. This fish was a trout.
I had seen enough of them to feel sure
of that. True, I had seen trout jump
out of the water, for a fly or to get up
over a waterfall; but I never before saw
a trout climb fifteen or twenty feet into
the air, over the tops of bushes and
young trees and land on the bank.

This was surely a matter that required explanation. An investigation was
necessary, and without hesitation I as-
sumed the role of sleuth. Carefully stepping out of the water, I sat on a rock
and took off my wading togs, then on
stockinged feet and on hands and knees
crept up the bank. Peering through the
bushes, I saw that since my last visit
a large birch tree had fallen across the
pool and that the trunk of this tree was
partly submerged. Sitting on this fallen

tree over the center of the pool was a large black bear. Her back was toward me, and she was in a stooping posture, holding one fore paw down in the water. I was just in time to see a sudden movement of the submerged paw and to see another trout, about twelve inches long, go sailing through the air and fall behind some bushes just beyond where I was in hiding. Rustling and squealing sounds coming from the direction in which the fish had gone, indicated that a pair of cubs were behind the bushes, and that they were scrapping over possession of the fish their mother had tossed up to them. It was, perhaps, ten minutes later I saw a third trout fly over the bushes toward the cubs. About this time the bear turned her head, sniffed the air in my direction, and with a low growl and a "Whoof," started briskly for shore, climbed the bank, collected the two cubs and made off into the woods, smashing brush and fallen limbs of trees, occasionally pausing to send back, in her own language, a remark indicating her disapproval of the party who had interrupted her fishing operations.

The mystery of the flying trout was now solved, but a new conundrum was presented to my enquiring mind; namely, how did the old lady catch them? With what did the bear bait her hooks?

I have told the story to many guides and woodsmen of my acquaintance, and from them have sought an answer to the question. Bige expressed the opinion that the bear dug worms, wedged them in between her toe-nails, and when the fish nibbled the worms the bear grabbed him. Frank referred to the well known pungent odor of the bear, especially of his feet, the tracks made by which a dog can smell hours, or even days after the bear has passed. He said that fish are attracted by the odor.

Also that many years ago, he had caught fish by putting oil of rhodium on the bait, and that "fish could smell it clear across the pond." Frank admitted that this method of fishing was not sportsman-like and that he had discontinued the practice. George said he had many times watched trout in a pool rub their sides against moss covered stones and often settle down upon the moss and rest there. He opined that they mistook the fur on the bear's paw for a particu-larly desirable variety of moss, and so were caught.

At this point in my investigations, I was reminded that a few years ago there was conducted, in the columns of several fishing and hunting magazines, a very serious discussion of the question, "Can fish be caught by tickling?" Many con-tributors took part in this discussion. There were advocates of both positive and negative side of the question. My old friend Hubbard, an expert fisherman, of wide experience, assured me that he, many years ago, had discarded the landing net; that when he hooked a lake trout, a bass or a "musky," and had played his fish until it was so exhausted that it could be reeled in and led up alongside the boat, it was his practice to "gently insert his hand in the water under the fish and tickle it on the the stomach, when the fish would settle down in his hand and go to sleep, then he would lift it into the boat."

This testimony took me back in memory to a time, many years ago, at a little red school house on the hill, in a New England country school district, where my young ideas took their first lessons in shooting. "Us fellers" then looked upon boys of twelve and thirteen years as the "big boys" of the school. We still believed in Santa Claus, and we knew that a bird could not be caught

58

An Expert Trout Fisher

without first "putting salt on its tail."
A brook crossed the road at the foot of
the hill and ran down through farmer
Barnum's pasture. In this brook, during the noon recess and after school had
closed for the day, with trousers rolled
up and with bare feet, we waded and
fished. We caught them with our hands,
and we kept them alive. Each boy had
his "spring hole," scooped out of the
sand near the edge of the stream, in
which he kept the fish caught. Of
course, whenever it rained, and the
water rose in the brook, these spring
holes were washed away and the fish
escaped. But when the waters sub-
sided, they had to be caught again.
Sometimes, we caught a chub as much
as four inches long; and on rare occasions, when a "horned dace, a five inch-
er" was secured, the boy who got him
was a hero. It was the firm conviction
of every boy in our gang, that, no matter

how securely a fish was cornered between the two hands and behind and under a sod or stone, he could not safely be lifted out of the water without first "tickling him on the belly."

Reverting to the suggestion made by Bige. There would be no doubt as to the bear's ability to dig worms. She is an expert digger, carries her garden tools with her. She has been known to dig a hole under a stump or rock, six or eight feet deep, in which she sleeps all winter. I have, myself, seen a bear dig wild turnips and have seen rotten stumps and logs torn to bits by their claws; which was done in a hunt for grubs. I therefore felt certain that if the bear dug any worms she would not use them for fish bait, but would herself eat them.

With a judicial attitude of mind, considering all the evidence submitted, including my own early experience, I have arrived at the conclusion that the trout was first attracted by the odor of the bear's paw, then rubbed against the soft fur, when the bear wiggled her toes and tickled the fish on his belly, whereupon the trout settled down in the bear's paw, went to sleep and was tossed up on the shore to the waiting cubs.

CPSIA information can be obtained at www.ICGtesting.com
Printed in the USA
LVOW11*1222010515

436838LV00008BA/34/P

9 781168 808127